What Would YOU Do?

Lincoln's Emancipation Proclamation

Would You Sign the Great Document?

Elaine Landau

Enslow Elementary

an imprint of

E **Enslow Publishers, Inc.**
40 Industrial Road
Box 398
Berkeley Heights, NJ 07922
USA

http://www.enslow.com

Enslow Elementary, an imprint of Enslow Publishers, Inc.

Enslow Elementary® is a registered trademark of Enslow Publishers, Inc.

Library of Congress Cataloging-in-Publication Data

Landau, Elaine.
   [Emancipation Proclamation]
   Lincoln's Emancipation Proclamation : would you sign the great document? / Elaine Landau.
     pages cm. — (What would you do?)
   "Originally published as The Emancipation Proclamation: Would You Do What Lincoln Did? in 2008"—Title page verso.
   Includes index.
   ISBN 978-0-7660-6290-0
   1. United States. President (1861–1865 : Lincoln). Emancipation Proclamation—Juvenile literature. 2. Lincoln, Abraham,
     1809-1865—Juvenile literature. 3. Slaves—Emancipation—United States—Juvenile literature. 4. United States—Politics
     and government—1861–1865—Juvenile literature. I. Title.
   E453.L25 2015
   973.7—dc23

                2014027417

Future editions:
Paperback ISBN: 978-0-7660-6291-7
EPUB ISBN: 978-0-7660-6292-4
Single Multi-User PDF ISBN: 978-0-7660-6293-1
Multi-User PDF ISBN: 978-0-7660-6294-8

Printed in the United States of America
102014 Bang Printing, Brainerd, Minn.
10 9 8 7 6 5 4 3 2 1

To Our Readers: We have done our best to make sure all Internet Addresses in this book were active and appropriate when we went to press. However, the author and the publisher have no control over and assume no liability for the material available on those Internet sites or on other Web sites they may link to. Any comments or suggestions can be sent by e-mail to comments@enslow.com or to the address on the back cover.

Every effort has been made to locate all copyright holders of material used in this book. If any errors or omissions have occurred, corrections will be made in future editions of this book.

Contents

Killed by a Mob

November 7, 1837, was a frightening day for newspaper editor Elijah Lovejoy. His new **printing press** had just arrived at a warehouse in Alton, Illinois. Now Lovejoy heard that a mob was coming to destroy it.

Lovejoy had good reason to be scared. Some people thought he was a troublemaker. Lovejoy hated slavery, and he had often spoken out against it in his newspaper.

This worried slave owners. At the time, slavery was legal in much of the United States. The slave owners wanted to keep it that way. They were determined to quiet Lovejoy for good.

In the past, slave owners had hired men to destroy three of Lovejoy's printing presses. However, this time Lovejoy was prepared for the mob. He, along with about twenty of his friends, stood guard at the warehouse. Those helping Lovejoy were firmly against slavery as well.

Before long, Lovejoy and his friends saw the mob coming down the road. They quickly saw that they were outnumbered. Some in the mob had firearms too.

Minutes later, the attack on the warehouse started. Men from the mob tried to place a ladder against the warehouse.

ALTON OBSERVER.
Extra.

ALTON, SEPTEMBER 28, 1837.

STATE CONVENTION.

The present aspect of the slavery question in this country, and especially in this State, is of commanding interest to us all. No question is, at the present time, exerting so strong an influence upon the public mind as this. The whole land is agitated by it. We cannot, nor would we remain indifferent spectators in the midst of developements so vitally interesting to us all, as those which are daily taking place in relation to the system of American Slavery.— We have duties to perform, as Christians and as Patriots, which call for united wisdom, counsel and energy of action.

The undersigned would, therefore, respectfully call a meeting of the friends of the slave and of free discussion in the State of Illinois, to meet in Convention at UPPER ALTON, ON THE LAST THURSDAY OF OCTOBER. It is intended that this Convention should consist of all those in the State who believe that the system of American Slavery is sinful and ought to be immediately abandoned, however diversified may be their views in other respects. It is desirable that the opponents in this State of Domestic Slavery—all who ardently long and pray to witness its *immediate* abolition, should co-operate together in their efforts

John E Morey
Peter M'Worthy
Bernard McKenzie
Porter Smith
A. C. Root
Artemas Ward
Charles Brown
Julius Brown
Elijah Ballard
Ebenezer White
Fairfield, Adams co.
J. B. Chittenden
W. H. Hubbard
William Kirby,
D. Bartholomew
Rufus Hubbard
Caleb Smith
Benjamin Baldwin
J. W. Cook
C. Talcott
Anson M. Hubbard
Chatham, Sangamon county.
L. N. Ransom
Josiah Porter
H. T. White
Cornelius Lyman
A. Stockwell
Peoria.
Jeremiah Porter,

Henry Ferris
Wm S Gale
James Waters
Samuel Hitchcock
Lucien Mills
George Ferris
Lorentus Conger
Henry Wilcox
Ephraim P Nail
Enos Pomeroy
John Waters
Geo. W. Gale,
Brainard Orton
Miles Smith
Hennepin.
W. M. Stuart
S. D. Laughlin
J. N. Laughlin
James G. Dunlavy
Stephen D. Willis
Springfield.
Erastus Wright
Z. Hallock
E. B. Hawley
R. P. Abel
Roswell Abel
W. M. Cowgill
Isaac Bancroft jr
J. C. Bancroft
Oliver B. Culver

Moses Forbes
S. E. Moore
E. Upham
James Mansfield
J. S. Clark
G. Holton
Rev. H. Loomis
J. Carpenter
E. Dennison
John Bates
H. Sterns
J. Thompson
Thomas Lippincott,
T. B. Hurlburt
F. W. Graves
Pleasant Grove, Taze-well co.
Julius Bascom
Washington, Tazewell co.
James P. Scott
F. R Whipple
Romulus Barnes
Sand Prairie, Tazewell co.
Lemuel Holton
Samuel C. Woodrow
Wm. Woodrow
H. D. Chipman
R. Grosvenor

Monmouth, Warren co
George H. Wright
Jacksonville.
Wm. Carter
E. Wolcott
Timothy Chamberlain
Thos W. Melendy
Jeremiah Graves
Maro M. L. Reed
C. B. Barton
J. G. Edwards
Martin Hart
C. B. Blood
F. W. Patterson
D. D. Nelson
W. Jones
M Hicks
W. T. Mills
A. B. Hitchcock
S. Wells
J. S. Graves
R. S. Kendall
E. Scofield
Lyman Harkness
R. M. Pearson
George Pyle
Thomas Lawrie
A. W. Estabrook
Ralph Perry
L. Dunham

On September 28, 1837, Elijah Lovejoy announced a meeting in the *Alton Observer*. The meeting was for a group that wanted to end slavery.

They hoped to climb to the top and set the roof on fire. Lovejoy and his friends tried to stop them.

Suddenly, shots rang out. Some in the mob had decided to use their guns instead of their fists. Lovejoy was hit five times and died on the spot.

Yet it was not over. The mob broke into the building. They smashed the printing press into pieces. Then they threw the pieces out of the window and dumped them into the river.

On November 7, 1837, an angry mob attacked Lovejoy's office and killed him. Although several people were arrested, none were found guilty of the crime.

In the mid-1800s, such violent clashes were common. Things were tense between the North and the South. Most of the slavery in the United States existed in the South. Much of the anger over slavery came from people in the North, like Elijah Lovejoy. At times, it felt as if the North and South were two separate countries.

Over the years, the areas had developed differently. The North had factories, **mills**, and shops. Northern cities were larger. People moved there to work in the factories. There were fewer family farms.

Newcomers had arrived from Europe. Many worked in Northern factories. Some started their own businesses.

Life in the South had a slower pace. The South had warm weather and rich soil. That made it ideal for farming.

All kinds of crops were grown there. The most important ones were tobacco, cotton, sugar, **indigo**, and rice. These were grown on large farms called **plantations**. Such crops brought high prices. Many Southern growers had become very wealthy.

Yet growing these crops was not easy. A lot of workers were needed. It would have been very costly to pay them all.

Therefore, growers bought slaves to work on their farms. The slaves were black men, women, and children. They were often brought to the United States by force. They came in chains on slave ships from Africa or were born to parents that were slaves in America. They were not paid for the work they did.

There were some slaves in the North. However, most were in the South.

In the 1800s, the North had more factories than the South.

There the slaves farmed the land. They also looked after the growers' homes and children.

A slave's life was hard. Most worked from sunup to sunset. They were given little to eat and hardly any clothes. They were often beaten as well.

Some Northerners, like Elijah Lovejoy, were very much against slavery. They felt that all human beings should be free. They did not want slavery in their country.

The Southern slave owners disagreed. They saw slaves as property. They wanted to keep their property.

Plantation owners used shackles to punish slaves and to keep them from running away. General Thomas F. Drayton of South Carolina had many slaves.

What Would YOU Do?

What if you were a governor in the South? You want to do your best for your state. You also want a united country. *Would you . . .*

❀ Vote for laws to limit farm size? Fewer large farms could mean fewer slaves. You could also urge businesses to come to the area.

❀ Help pass laws to change the plantation system? There would still be plantations, but workers would be paid. Owners would not make as much money, but there would be no slavery.

❀ Do nothing? You feel that government has no place in business. Besides, the state makes money by taxing plantations.

The South Keeps Slavery

Some of the South's governors were growers themselves. They did not try to change things.

That might have been a mistake. The divide between the North and South was growing. By the 1840s, even more people in the North wanted to end slavery.

There had already been some changes. Some Northern states outlawed slavery. Among these were New York, New Hampshire, New Jersey, and Vermont. There were others as well.

There had also been laws that changed the whole country. As early as 1808, the **United States Congress** had stopped the slave trade with other countries.

Slaves could no longer be brought to America from other places, including Africa. Yet slavery was still legal throughout the South. So the slave trade inside the United States went on.

After Congress stopped the slave trade, slaves could no longer be brought to America by ship.

The slaves living in the South had children. That kept the number of slaves growing. Both young and old slaves were still bought and sold.

What Would YOU Do?

What if you were a Northerner who had been elected to serve in the government? *Would you . . .*

❀ **See how unfair slavery is and fight for change?**

❀ **Go easy on the South? You do not want to anger half the nation.**

People Speak Out Against Slavery

Some Northern congressmen spoke out against slavery. More Northerners had grown tired of people being forced to work. They were ready for change.

Some people formed their own groups to stop slavery. They were known as **abolitionists**. They gave spirited speeches and held large meetings.

One abolitionist named Harriet Beecher Stowe wrote a book about slavery. It was called *Uncle Tom's Cabin*. It was very popular and caused many more people to want slavery to end.

The abolitionists also asked slaves to run away. At times, they hid slaves in their homes. They gave them food and money, too.

GEORGE PECK'S
GRAND REVIVAL OF
STETSON'S
UNCLE TOM'S CABIN

BOOKED BY
KLAW & ERLANGER

ELIZA   A·S·SEER'S
UNION SQUARE PRINT N.Y.

·UNCLE·TOM'S·CABIN·

116°

The book *Uncle Tom's Cabin* was written by Harriet Beecher Stowe (below). Stowe was against slavery. At the left is a picture of a character from the book named Eliza.

This made the Southern growers angry. They saw the abolitionist groups as the enemy. Some Southerners hired gangs of men to attack them. These slave owners were willing to use violence to make sure that slavery continued.

At times, abolitionist printing presses were destroyed. Slave owners did not want abolitionists printing flyers or

$200 Reward.

RANAWAY from the subscriber, on the night of Thursday, the 30th of Sepember,

FIVE NEGRO SLAVES,

To-wit: one Negro man, his wife, and three children.

The man is a black negro, full height, very erect, his face a little thin. He is about forty years of age, and calls himself *Washington Reed*, and is known by the name of Washington. He is probably well dressed, possibly takes with him an ivory headed cane, and is of good address. Several of his teeth are gone.

Mary, his wife, is about thirty years of age, a bright mulatto woman, and quite stout and strong.

The oldest of the children is a boy, of the name of FIELDING, twelve years of age, a dark mulatto, with heavy eyelids. He probably wore a new cloth cap.

MATILDA, the second child, is a girl, six years of age, rather a dark mulatto, but a bright and smart looking child.

MALCOLM, the youngest, is a boy, four years old, a lighter mulatto than the last, and about equally as bright. He probably also wore a cloth cap. If examined, he will be found to have a swelling at the navel.

Washington and Mary have lived at or near St. Louis, with the subscriber, for about 15 years.

It is supposed that they are making their way to Chicago, and that a white man accompanies them, that they will travel chiefly at night, and most probably in a covered wagon.

A reward of $150 will be paid for their apprehension, so that I can get them, if taken within one hundred miles of St. Louis, and $200 if taken beyond that, and secured so that I can get them, and other reasonable additional charges, if delivered to the subscriber, or to THOMAS ALLEN, Esq., at St. Louis, Mo. The above negroes, for the last few years, have been in possession of Thomas Allen, Esq., of St. Louis.

WM. RUSSELL.

ST. LOUIS, Oct. 1, 1847.

Slaves often tried to run away from their owners' plantations. This poster is an ad a slave owner published, which offered a reward for the return of his slaves.

newspaper articles against slavery. Some abolitionists were badly beaten as well. A few were even killed.

Angry planters were not the only problem. Not everyone in the North wanted slavery to end. Some did not want the freed slaves coming north. They feared that they might take their jobs.

These people could try to cause harm too. They would sometimes come to antislavery meetings. However, they were there to hurt the speakers.

What Would YOU Do?

What if you were fighting to stop slavery? Now your life may be at risk. *Would you . . .*

❁ **Fight harder than ever? Your work is too important to stop.**

❁ **Step away from the fight? Your safety is important as well.**

Abolitionists Keep Fighting

The abolitionists believed that the United States could never truly be free while there were slaves. They felt that few things were as important as freedom.

Some abolitionists became more active. Like Stowe, they wrote books and plays against slavery. They put out their own newspapers, too. Frederick Douglass published a newspaper called *The North Star*. Many went from state to state speaking against slavery.

Frederick Douglass was an escaped slave who wanted to end slavery.

THE NORTH STAR.

Douglass's first autobiography, published in 1845, was a powerful account of slavery. In 1847, he started *The North Star,* a newspaper filled with articles against slavery.

A number of abolitionists were African Americans. Some were freed slaves. Others, like Douglass, had escaped from the South.

The Southern growers feared the abolitionists. They had other fears, too. In 1860, Abraham Lincoln was running for president. Lincoln was the choice of the **Republican Party**. The South did not see him as a friend.

The country was growing. Settlers were heading west. Lincoln did not want the West to have slaves.

The South was against this. The farmers did not want slavery limited. They believed not letting new states have slavery could lead to the end of slavery in all the states.

Southern leaders threatened to take action if Lincoln was elected president. Some states were prepared to break away and form their own nation. Then Lincoln was elected the sixteenth president of the United States.

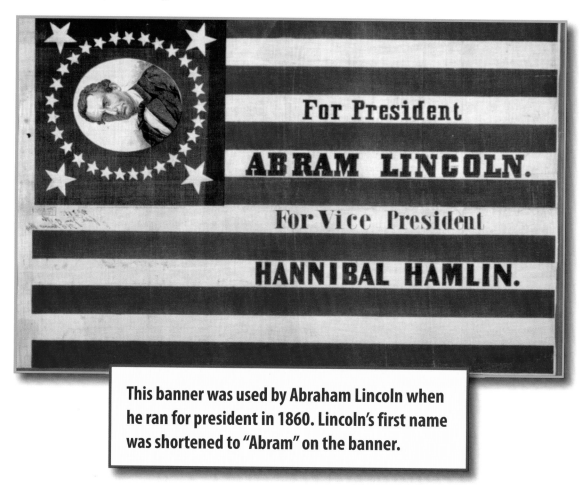

For President

ABRAM LINCOLN.

For Vice President

HANNIBAL HAMLIN.

This banner was used by Abraham Lincoln when he ran for president in 1860. Lincoln's first name was shortened to "Abram" on the banner.

In 1860, Abraham Lincoln (left) was elected the sixteenth president of the United States of America. John C. Breckenridge (right) received the most votes in the southern states. However, he was unable to beat Lincoln.

What Would YOU Do?

What if you were a Southern leader?
Would you . . .

❀ Urge the South to leave the United States? If you had your own country, Northerners could not tell you how to live.

❀ Tell people to stay calm? You love the United States. You do not want to see it divided. You try to work things out with those in the North.

Southern States Leave the Union

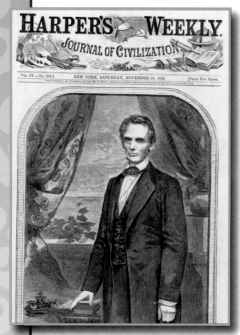

The Southern leaders kept their word. They decided to leave the Union, which was what the United States was sometimes called. They felt that they had to do this to keep their way of life. They wanted to keep slavery in the South.

South Carolina was the first state to go in December 1860. Five others soon followed. In February 1861, six states formed a new country. It was called the Confederate States of America.

The cover of the November 10, 1860, issue of *Harper's Weekly* announced that Lincoln had become president.

Five more Southern states soon followed their lead. Before long, much of the South had left the Union. The nation had been split apart.

The South set up a government. It also formed an army and navy. **Rebels** stood ready to fight for their new nation.

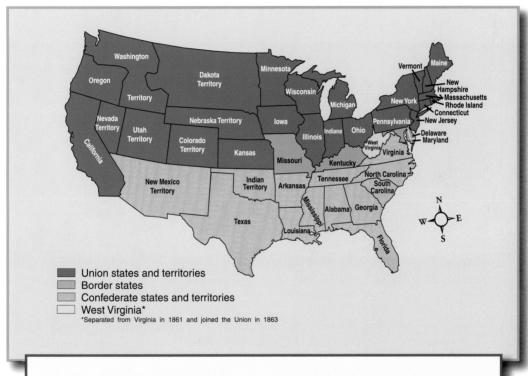

A map of the United States at the time of the Civil War shows the Union and Confederate states and territories. The border states remained part of the Union; many of them still had slavery. West Virginia broke away from Confederate Virginia in 1861 to become its own state in the Union.

The South was bold. It began taking over Union property. Then on April 12, 1861, it made its most daring move. It attacked Fort Sumter in South Carolina. Fort Sumter was a Union fort.

Now President Lincoln had a hard choice to make. He had to defend the Union. Yet that would mean going to war.

The South attacked Fort Sumter in South Carolina's Charleston Harbor. The battle began on April 12, 1861, and ended the next day.

What Would YOU Do?

What if you were President Lincoln's adviser?
Would you . . .

✳ Tell him to go to war? He must defeat the South at once.

✳ Urge Lincoln to stay calm? A war will be costly. Too many Americans will die.

✳ Tell Lincoln to free the slaves at once? The South will suffer without them. Besides, the freed slaves could join the Union army. That would help in a war.

Lincoln's advisers sit around him. What would you say if you were one of them?

Abe Lincoln Goes to War

President Lincoln went to war. Yet he did not free the slaves right away. There was a reason for that.

Lincoln wanted the South to come back to the Union. If slavery was outlawed, the South might not come back. Also, some states near the border of the North and South still had slaves. But they had stayed with the Union. Lincoln did not want to upset these states.

President Lincoln decided to go to war after the South attacked Fort Sumter.

The South's defeat at Fort Donelson on February 16, 1862, was the North's first major victory of the Civil War.

Lincoln also did not want to upset the Union soldiers. These men were fighting to save the Union. They did not want their country torn apart. Many might have thought that slavery was unfair, but not every northerner would risk his life to end it.

General Robert E. Lee led the Confederate forces.

By 1862, the North was in trouble. Robert E. Lee was a great Confederate general. He led his troops well. The South had defeated the North in many battles.

Lee drove the Union army out of south Virginia. President Lincoln was afraid the South might win the war.

The North badly needed more soldiers. Lincoln thought about freeing the slaves. They could join the Union army. The South would also lose its free labor.

In July 1862, President Lincoln made an important decision and wrote it down. It was called the Emancipation Proclamation. It freed the slaves in the states that were still at war with the United States.

Lincoln read it to his advisers. He wanted to know what they thought. Should he free these slaves?

What Would YOU Do?

What if you had to advise Lincoln?
Would you . . .

✿ Tell him to free the slaves at once?

✿ Ask Lincoln to wait? The South has won too many battles. Freeing the slaves now would make the North look scared.

The first reading of the Emancipation Proclamation before Lincoln's advisers, who were also called his Cabinet.

The Slaves Are Not Freed Right Away

President Lincoln's advisers told him to wait. Making the Emancipation Proclamation public in July 1862 would look bad. The North needed to win an important battle first.

Lincoln took their advice. He did not want to make a mistake this early in the war. Too much was at stake.

The Battle of Antietam was the bloodiest single-day battle ever fought in the United States. Many soldiers on each side died.

Abraham Lincoln waited for a victory on the battlefield. On September 17, 1862, it happened. The South invaded Maryland. The two sides fought at Antietam Creek.

The fighting lasted all day. Men on both sides died. Yet in the end, the North won.

The victory meant a lot to President Lincoln. Now he revealed the Emancipation Proclamation to the public.

Above, Lincoln is pictured with Allan Pinkerton (left), a Union spy, and Major General John A. McClernand (right), after the Battle of Antietam.

The South now had until January 1, 1863, to return. If it did not, the Southern slaves would be freed.

The Emancipation Proclamation would not free all slaves. Only slaves that lived in states or parts of states still at war with the Union would be freed. Slaves in parts of the country that never went to war or had given up would not be freed.

The same was true for slave owners in Maryland, Delaware, Missouri, and Kentucky. These states bordered the South. However, they had never left the Union. Slave owners there could keep their slaves too.

Above are the first and last pages of an original draft of Lincoln's Emancipation Proclamation. The last page has a seal on it. A seal was used along with a signature to prove someone had signed a document.

In this painting, an African-American man reads a newspaper with the headline, "Presidential Proclamation, Slavery," which refers to the Emancipation Proclamation.

Some Northerners felt this was wrong. They were against slavery. They wanted to see all the slaves freed.

What Would YOU Do?

What if you were the president? *Would you . . .*

✿ Free all the slaves? It does not matter if some Southerners were loyal. Slavery is wrong.

✿ Only free the slaves in the rebel states? You do not want to anger loyal Southerners. They might side with the South instead. Then the Union could lose the war.

Only Slaves in Rebel States Are Freed

Lincoln left the Emancipation Proclamation as it was. Only slaves in rebel states would be freed. This way states that had remained loyal to the Union would not be punished. They would continue to side with the North.

The Southern growers were very upset. So was Jefferson Davis. He was the president of the Confederate States. Davis felt that Lincoln had no right to set the slaves free.

The Emancipation Proclamation would free the slaves in all states still in rebellion. African-American families like this one would be free as soon as President Lincoln signed the proclamation.

To Davis, the Confederacy was its own nation. He believed it no longer had to follow the laws of the Union.

Also, the promise of freedom would give the slaves hope. Davis saw that as a dangerous idea. They might rebel against their owners.

Jefferson Davis was the president of the Confederacy.

What Would YOU Do?

What if you were Jefferson Davis? *Would you . . .*

✺ Urge the South to fight harder than ever? You do not trust Lincoln. You want to be sure that slavery continues in the South.

✺ Accept Lincoln's offer to return to the Union? A lot of lives will be saved if the fighting stops. You believe Lincoln's promise. Slave owners will be able to keep their slaves if they return to the Union.

Here's what happened:

The South Battles On

The South refused to return to the Union. It kept on fighting. Many in the South still hoped to win the war. Besides, if the South returned to the Union, some felt that slavery would probably be outlawed in the future. Most Southerners just ignored the Emancipation Proclamation.

This discouraged some in the North. These people were not abolitionists. They did not care about slavery.

African-American men, women, and children gather around a man with a watch, waiting for the Emancipation Proclamation to take effect. Gatherings like this were called "watch meetings."

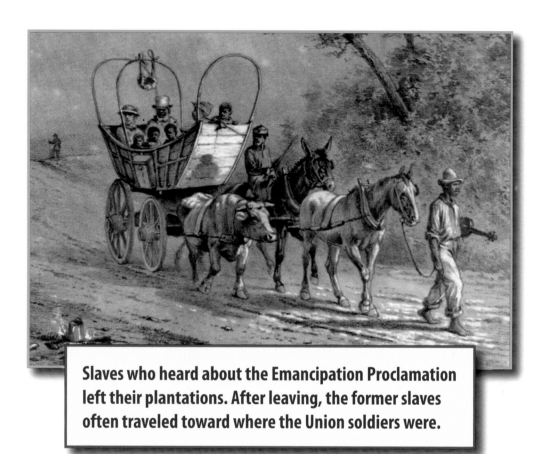

Slaves who heard about the Emancipation Proclamation left their plantations. After leaving, the former slaves often traveled toward where the Union soldiers were.

They urged Lincoln to give up on the Emancipation Proclamation. They were tired of fighting. They just wanted the South to come back to the Union.

However, on January 1, 1863, Lincoln signed the Emancipation Proclamation. That made it law.

Slave owners tried to hide this from their slaves. Yet word of it spread. Large numbers of slaves soon learned they were free.

Lincoln signed the Emancipation Proclamation on January 1, 1863.

The growers warned them not to leave. They were serious about this. They swore that they would catch and kill any runaway slaves.

Many slaves still tried to escape. At times, these slaves reached Union army camps. These camps were spread throughout the land in the South that the Union army had captured.

Often escaped slaves asked the Union soldiers for help. Many had left their families behind. It was much too hard for large groups of slaves to escape at once.

Now escaped slaves wanted the soldiers to go back with them. They hoped the Union soldiers could free their loved ones.

But the Union army was short of men. There was little time to go to plantations. That would not be an easy task either.

The soldiers would have to face groups of angry slave owners. Many growers were armed and ready to fight for their property. Some wanted to keep their slaves at any cost. However, many growers were off fighting the war as well.

What Would YOU Do?

What if you were a captain in the Union army? *Would you . . .*

❀ Refuse to help the slaves? Your men are tired. Quite a few have been wounded. They need to save their strength for battle.

❀ Send a few men out? You believe in freedom for everyone. Maybe some of the slaves will join the Union army. You badly need more soldiers.

The Union Army Helps Some Slaves

At times, Union soldiers helped free slaves. These newly freed slaves often joined the Union army. This increased the Union's fighting power.

However, such army trips to plantations did not happen very often. Usually, there was not enough extra time or extra men to do this. For the most part, slaves were on their own.

Many slaves escaped with no help from the Union Army. Sometimes slaves got lost in the swamps of the South.

At first, it was hard for any slave to leave. The growers were armed—the slaves were not. The Emancipation Proclamation sounded great. Yet for many slaves, it did not mean freedom.

But escapes became more common. Some slaves felt even more daring. They sensed that freedom was near.

Some former slaves made it to the Union Army camps. There, they helped the soldiers.

What Would YOU Do?

What if you were a slave? *Would you . . .*

✺ **Try to get to a Union army camp?** You could sign up. It would be your first paying job.

✺ **Try to escape to the North?** You could start a new life there.

✺ **Hide out in the South?** Stay in the forests and swamps until the war was over.

Former Slaves Join the Union Cause

Many escaped slaves joined the Union army. Almost two hundred thousand of them signed up. They fought hard as soldiers. They knew how important winning was.

Slaves helped the Union army in other ways, too. Some worked for the troops for food or money. Women and children cooked and did laundry. At times, slaves made excellent scouts because they knew the area so well.

Former slaves joined the Union Army and fought bravely in many Civil War battles.

Fewer slaves made it to the North. Some small groups of slaves also hid out in the South.

The loss of these slaves hurt the South. Growers were short of help. They could not produce enough food for the South's army.

The Emancipation Proclamation helped the Union in other ways too. Now the countries of England and France did not think the South was its own nation. They refused to give the South money or guns.

In 1864, President Lincoln put General Ulysses S. Grant in command of all Union forces. Grant proved to be a worthy match for General Robert E. Lee. Grant pushed his men hard to win.

General Ulysses S. Grant led the Union Army to many great victories.

As the months passed, the South grew weaker. By February 1865, its army was doing poorly. Many of the men had been killed or wounded.

Union troops had taken over Southern plantations and cities. Now large numbers of slaves on the plantations and in other places in the South were freed.

Even the border states faced the truth. The time for slavery was over. If slavery was outlawed in the South, it would probably soon be outlawed throughout the nation. They knew they would have to give up their slaves.

Lincoln now wanted the nation to be truly free. He did not want slavery in any part of it. That would mean changing the **Constitution**—the laws governing America.

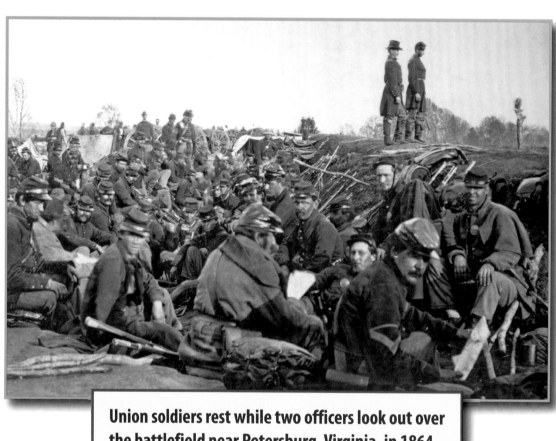

Union soldiers rest while two officers look out over the battlefield near Petersburg, Virginia, in 1864.

An **amendment** is a change to a document. Congress came up with a Thirteenth Amendment, to the Constitution. It would outlaw slavery in the United States for good. President Lincoln urged Congress to pass it. The Thirteenth Amendment would make the United States a truly free country.

This is a copy of the Emancipation Ordinance of Missouri, which freed the slaves in that state on January 11, 1865. Lincoln's Emancipation Proclamation had not freed the slaves in Missouri since it had never left the Union.

What Would YOU Do?

What if you were a member of Congress?
Would you . . .

❀ Outlaw slavery in the United States? It has no place in a free nation.

❀ Vote against outlawing it? You do not want to be too hard on the South. The Southerners already feel beaten down.

All the Slaves Are Freed

Congress passed the Thirteenth Amendment. On December 18, 1865, the amendment became law. Now slavery was illegal throughout the United States.

But before this, on April 9, 1865, General Robert E. Lee had already surrendered. The Civil War had ended. The Southern states returned to the Union.

Lincoln's Emancipation Proclamation was written to save the Union. But it did much more than that. It helped make every American truly free.

African-American soldiers helped the Union win the Civil War.

Timeline

1808—Congress stops the U.S. slave trade with other countries.

1830s—Tensions between the North and South grow over slavery.

1860—Abraham Lincoln is elected president of the United States; some Southern states begin to leave the Union.

1861—*February:* Six Southern states form a new nation called the Confederate States of America; more Southern states leave the Union to join them.

April 12: Confederates attack Fort Sumter; the Civil War begins.

1862—*July:* Lincoln writes the Emancipation Proclamation.

September 17: Union forces win the battle at Antietam; Lincoln announces the Emancipation Proclamation.

1863—*January 1:* Lincoln signs the Emancipation Proclamation. It is now law.

1864—Lincoln puts General Ulysses S. Grant in command of all Union forces.

1865—*February:* The South is doing poorly in the war.

April 9: The South surrenders; the Civil War is over.

December 6: The Thirteenth Amendment outlaws slavery in the United States.

Words to Know

abolitionist—A person who worked to end slavery.

amendment—A change made to a body of laws.

constitution—The body of rules and laws that tells how a government is organized.

emancipation—To be freed from slavery.

governor—The leader of a state.

indigo—A plant with deep purple berries. Indigo is used to make a dark blue dye.

mill—A factory with machinery for making cloth, paper, or other products.

plantation—A large farm in a warm climate where such crops as cotton and tobacco are grown.

printing press—A machine used to print words on paper for newspapers, flyers, and other items.

rebel—To fight against the government or a person who fights against the government.

Republican Party—One of the main political parties in the United States.

United States Congress—The government of the United States.

Learn More

Books

Hale, Sarah Elder, ed. *Abraham Lincoln: Defender of the Union.* Peterborough, N.H.: Cobblestone, 2005.

Hossel, Karen Price. *Emancipation Proclamation.* Chicago: Heinemann Library, 2006.

King, Wilma. *Children of the Emancipation.* Minneapolis, Minn.: Carolrhoda Books, 2000.

McComb, Marianne. *The Emancipation Proclamation.* Washington, D.C.: National Geographic, 2006.

Pickney, Andrea Davis. *Abraham Lincoln: Letters From a Slave Girl.* Delray Beach, Fla.: Winslow, 2001.

Internet Addresses

Ben's Guide to U.S. Government for Kids: The Emancipation Proclamation
<http://bensguide.gpo.gov/3-5/documents/proclamation/index.html>
Read the Emancipation Proclamation and learn all about this historic document and President Abraham Lincoln.

Abraham Lincoln
<http://www.socialstudiesforkids.com/subjects/abrahamlincoln.htm>
Just click any of the links to learn more about Abraham Lincoln.

Index